Behind *the* Scenes

at the TV News Studio

by **Marilyn Miller**
illustrated by **Ingo Fast**

®
RSVP
**RAINTREE
STECK-VAUGHN**
P U B L I S H E R S
The Steck-Vaughn Company

Austin, Texas

Published by Raintree Steck-Vaughn Publishers,
an imprint of Steck-Vaughn Company
Developed for Steck-Vaughn Company by
Visual Education Corporation, Princeton, New Jersey
Project Director: Paula McGuire
Production Supervision: Barbara A. Kopel
Electronic Preparation: Cynthia C. Feldner
Art Director: Maxson Crandall

Raintree Steck-Vaughn Publishers staff
Editor: Pamela Wells
Project Manager: Joyce Spicer

Library of Congress Cataloging-in-Publication Data
Miller, Marilyn F.
Behind the scenes at the TV news studio / Marilyn F. Miller :
illustrated by Ingo Fast.
p. cm.—
Includes bibliographical references (p.) and index.
Summary: A behind-the-scenes account of activities of a television newsroom such as conducting interviews, editing film footage, and working in the control room.
ISBN 0-8172-4089-6
1. Television broadcasting of news—United States—Juvenile literature.
[1. Television broadcasting of news.]   I. Fast, Ingo, ill.   II. Title.
PN4888.T4M475   1996
070.1´95—dc20   95-19525   CIP   AC

Printed and bound in the United States
1 2 3 4 5 6 7 8 9 0   IP   99 98 97 96 95

Table of Contents

The World of TV News. 4

Planning a News Program. 6

On Location 8

Meet the Press 10

From Videotape to Story 12

Putting the Pieces Together 14

The Talent 16

Final Touches 18

The Sports Desk. 20

The Weather Report 22

Bulletin!. 24

News Central 26

On the Air! 28

Glossary 30

Further Readings. 31

Index 32

Come visit behind the scenes of a television newsroom. Look inside and see how everything works.

Planning a News Program

People watch TV news programs to find out what is happening in the world. Each morning the news staff meets to plan the day's program.

Editors list the stories that will be part of the news for that day. They always do this before the story meeting. Information comes by fax, telephone, computer, and satellite.

Do you see the editor in the vest? He is directing the meeting. He asks if any other stories should be added. Reporters are told which stories to cover. They will find out what is happening and write the news stories.

Here is an assistant buying newspapers and magazines. These are for reporters and editors to read. They may find another story to report on.

On Location

TV reporters often interview people on location. This is outside the studio, where the action takes place. Reporters often carry their own video cameras to shoot what's happening. Other times, a cameraperson videotapes the story or the interview.

Do you see the reporter interviewing a woman? Sometimes, a crowd gathers during an interview. People like to jump in front of the camera and wave.

Most TV news stories take up only a few minutes on the news show. Each story must report only the most important information— that is, the **five W's.** People need to know **w**hat happened, **w**ho it happened to, **w**here it happened, **w**hen it happened, and **w**hy it happened.

Sometimes, reporters use the TV studio's van to go to an interview.

Meet the Press

The mayor has something important to announce. He wants to meet with the press. His office calls the TV news studio. The editor learns what will be said. He sends one special reporter to cover the story.

Radio, newspaper, and magazine reporters and camera people also come. Do you see the mayor behind the microphones? He is answering the reporters' questions.

Here is a reporter showing his identification (ID) to a security person at the mayor's office.

Find the reporter raising her camera above her head.

From Videotape to Story

The reporter and the editor work on the story. They use editing machines to help them put together the pictures and the sound from the videotape. The machines also help make sure that the story is long enough or short enough.

Do you see the reporter and the editor? They are watching the final videotape. They are looking for some sound bites. These are short, interesting statements made by people in the news story.

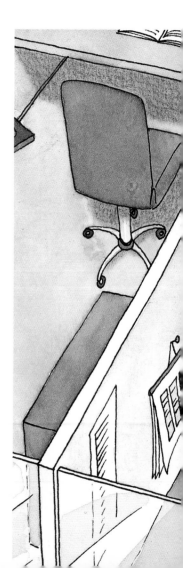

At last, the editor and the reporter have completed the tape. Here's the editor carrying the videotaped story to the producer. The producer will decide how to fit the story into the news program.

Putting the Pieces Together

Do you see the reporter typing the word "news" on the electronic letter-making machine? It makes all the words and names that appear on the TV screen during the news show.

Editors use computers to make special pictures or other art for programs. For example, such a picture may always be used at the beginning of the program. People then know right away that the news is coming on.

Here is a reporter on location writing her story. When the story is taped, she will try not to look down at her words. She will know her story and look right at the camera.

The Talent

Do you see the two anchors at the newsroom's anchor desk? They are called co-anchors. They usually take turns introducing the day's stories. Most anchors start out as TV reporters.

Sometimes, anchors may ask questions of a reporter doing a live interview. A live interview is one that is happening at the same time as the news show.

Here is an anchor reading a news story from a machine called a prompter. It shows her what words to say.

Final Touches

Do you see the makeup person checking to see that the anchor's hair looks right? The makeup person may also put makeup on the anchor's face. The makeup hides wrinkles, freckles, or shadows under the eyes.

Sometimes, anchors may sweat under the hot TV lights. The makeup person knows how to make them look dry. The makeup person always makes sure that all members of the news team look natural and healthy.

A small microphone is attached to the clothing of each person on the news team. That way, viewers can hear what each one is saying.

Here is an assistant checking the lights. They should be right on the anchors.

The Sports Desk

The sports reporter gives the scores of the day's most important sports events. He or she often goes to a big game. There, the most exciting plays are shot on videotape. The reporter can show these plays while describing them to viewers.

Do you see the reporter asking a player questions? The most interesting things the player says may also appear on the show.

Here is a family looking at the sports news in a restaurant. The sports report is one of the most popular parts of TV news.

The Weather Report

TV weather reporters tell what the weather is that day. They also say what the weather will be like for the next few days.

Do you see the weather reporter? The weather map is already on the viewer's TV screen at home.

A computer then puts the image of the reporter together with the weather map. The reporter can see herself on a separate screen. That way, she can decide how to point things out on the map.

Weather reporters receive information from weather services. The United States government tells them about the most recent weather in the area or over the whole country.

Here is the weather reporter in front of a weather map on her computer screen. Weather maps are made from information collected from all over the world.

Bulletin!

Do you see the reporter on location in Egypt? She is reporting a discovery made at a pyramid. Her TV equipment is connected to a station nearby.

The station sends the report to a satellite high above the earth. The satellite sends the report to the home station's control room. Here, the producer and the director put the story on the air.

Often, the home station sends a story to other U.S. stations around the country. The story is sent by cable or satellite.

Here is an anchor entering a helicopter. She will report on a story far away from the studio.

News Central

After videotaping, the reporter edits, or cuts, the story. The story has to fit the time allowed for it on the show.

The director puts together the whole news show in the control room. Here, many TV screens show pictures from each videotape that will be used during the program.

The director chooses each picture that will be shown on TV during the show. Many times, the reporter will also add the voice, or sound track, to the story.

One worker is looking for a tape to use on the show. Where is that person?

Here are the experts near the TV sets. They make sure that the news show looks and sounds good.

How many workers are using computers?

On the Air!

Do you see the co-anchors on the TV screen? The producer is in charge of the show when it is on. He or she tells the anchors what story is next. The producer also tells which cameras will show the anchors, sports reporters, or others on the news team.

Why don't viewers hear the producer telling people what to do? All the members of the news team wear a pair of small earphones. That way, they are the only ones who hear the producer.

Sometimes, reporters are on the scene of a story that is happening at the same time as the show. The producer makes sure that the anchors and the viewers can hear the reporters.

The producer decides when to show commercials. They are usually put in at certain times, such as every ten minutes. The commercials are made by another company and are sent to the station.

Here is the producer showing the anchor that the show is about to start.

Glossary

The **anchor** introduces each story. Two anchors on the same show are called **co-anchors.**

The **control room** is where the show is put together.

The **director** puts the news show together in the control room.

The **five W's** are the most important parts of the story. They tell **w**hat happened, **w**ho it happened to, **w**here it happened, **w**hen it happened, and **w**hy it happened.

The **makeup person** puts makeup on the news team's faces. This makes them look natural on camera.

On location is when the reporter goes outside the studio. He or she reports on the story from where it takes place.

The **producer** is in charge of the show.

Sound bites are short and interesting statements made by people in the news story.

The **sports reporter** tells about the day's most important sports stories.

The **story meeting** is a daily meeting. Here reporters learn which story they will cover.

The **weather reporter** tells what the weather will be for the next few days.

Further Readings

Freed, Carol. *Let's Visit a TV Station.* Mahwah, New Jersey: Troll, 1988.

Gesler, Ingrid. *TV and Video.* Ada, Oklahoma: Garrett, 1991.

Scott, Elaine. *Behind the Scenes of a Television Show.* New York: Morrow, 1988.

Trainer, David. *A Day in the Life of a TV News Reporter.* Mahwah, New Jersey: Troll, 1980.

Index

anchor 16, 17, 18, 19, 25, 28, 29
assistants 7, 19

cable 25
cameraperson 8, 11
cameras 8, 11, 15, 17
co-anchors 16, 28
commercial 29
computer 6, 13, 15, 23, 27
control room 24, 26

director 24, 26, 27

earphones 28
editing machines 12
editors 6, 7, 10, 12, 13, 15
Egypt 24

fax 6
five W's 9

makeup person 18, 19
mayor's press conference 10, 11
microphones 11, 19

on location 8, 9, 15, 24

producer 13, 24, 28, 29
prompter 17

reporters 7, 8, 9, 10, 11, 12, 13, 14,
    15, 16, 17, 20, 21, 23, 24, 27, 28

satellite 6, 24, 25
sound bites 12
soundtrack 27
sports reporter 20, 28
story meeting 6

TV lights 19
TV screen 14, 22

video cameras 8
videotapes 8, 12, 15, 20, 26
viewers 20, 28

weather map 22, 23
weather reporter 22, 23
weather service 23